Other books by Tom Leech a versatile author

Titillating Tales from the Outhouse, and
other perky poetic adventures.
Presentations Press, 2020

Fun on the Job: Amusing and true tales from Rosie-the Riveters
to Rocket Scientists at a Major Aerospace Company.
Presentations Press, 2017

The Curious Adventures of Santa's Wayward Elves
with Leslie Johnson- Leech.
Presentations Press 2014

Say it like Shakespeare: The Bard's Timeless Tips
for Communication Success
2nd Ed.
Presentations Press 2013 (Previously published in 2001
by McGraw-Hill)

On the Road in '68: a year of turmoil, a journey of friendship.
Presentations Press 2009.

Outdoors San Diego: Hiking, Biking and **Camping**
(with Jack Farnan), Premier 2004

How to Prepare, Stage & Deliver Winning Presentations,
3rd *Edition,*
AMACOM American Management Association) 2004
(1st Edition 1982)

TOM'S POETRY,
FROM BACK WHEN TO RIGHT NOW

TOM LEECH

Copyright © 2022, 2024 Tom Leech.

All rights reserved. No part of this book may be reproduced, stored, or transmitted by any means—whether auditory, graphic, mechanical, or electronic—without written permission of both publisher and author, except in the case of brief excerpts used in critical articles and reviews. Unauthorized reproduction of any part of this work is illegal and is punishable by law.

This is a work of fiction. Names, characters, places and incidents either are the product of the author's imagination or are used fictitiously, and any resemblance to any actual persons, living or dead, events, or locales is entirely coincidental.

ISBN: 979-8-89419-560-5 (sc)
ISBN: 979-8-89419-561-2 (hc)
ISBN: 979-8-89419-562-9 (e)

Because of the dynamic nature of the Internet, any web addresses or links contained in this book may have changed since publication and may no longer be valid. The views expressed in this work are solely those of the author and do not necessarily reflect the views of the publisher, and the publisher hereby disclaims any responsibility for them.

One Galleria Blvd., Suite 1900, Metairie, LA 70001
(504) 702-6708

"Tom Leech's poetry is a treasure trove of gentle recollections, back porch wisdom and sly humor. A gentle volume of poetry, filled with rhyming recollections, back porch wisdom and just plain fun."

—**Corey Lynn Fayman,** award-winning author
of the *Rolly Waters Mystery* series

"Tom Leech's From Back When to Right Now is a glimpse of nostalgia, a wink to the future, and a feel-good dose of down-home humor that makes the puzzle pieces just click together. A very fine read, indeed."

—**M. Lee Buompensiero,** award-winning author of *Sumerland*

"This volume represents the distilled wisdom of a special poet, a friend of astronauts and rocket scientists, a soul overflowing with boundless curiosity. It's the work of an adventurer with a keen gift of observation and a genius for context. He's in awe of Shakespeare, seasoned with a pinch of Ogden Nash. Despite his world perspective, he's a Norman Rockwell using verse instead of paint. He's an American in Paris who still remembers the day that Harry Truman came to his Indiana hometown. And he'll make you remember it, too."

—**Phil Oakley,** Author of *Telegraph and the
Morello Family* series of crime novels

Contents

With Appreciation ix

GROWING UP

Where's My Front Porch? 2
"Ma, There's A Hobo At The Door" 3
Tackling Life's Early Dilemmas 5
Kids Buying Bonds? 7
The Iceman, The Milkman And The Mailman 9
Slidin' down Milks Hill 11
It's Scramble Time When The Soot Hits The Sheets 13
Shoes? Who Needs Shoes? 15
Saturday Night With The Monsters 17
I Never Peed In The Pool 19

HISTORICAL MOMENTS FROM MY EARLY YEARS

Saturday Bath On The Farm 22
When Peanuts Blair Was On the Mound 24
Baldy at the Bat 27
The Day Old Harry Came to Garrett 30
The Legend Of Emily Morgan: The Real Yellow Rose? 33
Pair Up for Fame 36

TALES ABOUT FRIENDS AND FAMILY

Strain Behind The Plate 40
Tom Fleming Moves On 43

Hot Curl – The Surfing Legend Of Windansea.....................44
The Legend of Hot Curl..45
Ah Those Memorable Beach Hangouts..........................50
What's more awesome than a butterfly?..........................52
Great Duos of History..53
It's a Trio World..55
Quartets Abound...57
Nature the Rejuvenator..59
Presidio Park: How We Got A Fun Park For Free 61
The Next Time Around – Transmigration 63
What's That Word Again?
How The Farm Boy Pursues The Chicks...........................65

CELEBRATING OUR MODERN TIMES

The Seven Days Of San Diego Christmas...........................68
The Night The Reindeer Stayed Home.............................70
Deck the Halls – the Kitchen Calls..................................73
The Ode to Murphy..74
Getting The Straight Poop For Those Special Reserved Seats 76
Where Does Santa Go?..79

THE WORLD WE LIVE IN, PLUS OR MINUS

Adding To Your Communication Success: Per The Bard's Tips 82
Hawaii Workout: (Oral Exercise) 84
Golf And English Are Tricky Games.................................85
Ode To A Titian Urn (Or Let's Hear It For The Chamberpot).......87
They're Better Than Us – Hah!......................................90

With Appreciation

Key to making this set of poetic tales as a book was initially the many connections I've had from day one with immediate family and various kinfolk: aunts, uncles, and cousins. Fun poetic tales were regular parts of our family gatherings and chit chats in our small town and country locations back home again in Indiana. Also stimulating my regular poetic outbursts were lots of friends in school and other locales, plus work and fun roundups in more vintage years. So thanks to all those stimulators for these many poetic tales. And thanks to my frequent book content and layout supporter, Patsy Powell Corlett.

GROWING UP

Where's My Front Porch?

By Tom Leech
From *The Guilded Pen* 2020 Anthology of
San Diego Writers & Editors Guild

Houses today lack one special pleasure,
They have doors and roofs and maybe a scenic torch,
Driveways, garages and good-looking eaves,
But what's generally missing is there's no front porch.

Houses today do make living OK,
Just walk on up the steps and right there's the front door,
Insert your key and then wander on in,
That's about the same whether you're rich or you're poor.

But a house with a front porch expands your life,
You can sit there and be a loafer or greeter,
Maybe read today's paper or a fun book,
Or enjoy hummingbirds slurping at your feeder.

Sit on a couch and peruse your own world,
Check out that big old tree and the joy it does bring,
Say hello to a passing-by neighbor,
Who might just stroll on up and join you on the swing.

It adds some cheer as you chat about stuff,
Gossip about the preacher or your friend's new pup,
How the local school ball team did last night,
Or what the mayor and council are messing up.

How engage the neighbors or flop on the swing,
If you have no front porch to share worry or cheer?
So, call your builder and say "Make me a porch,
To enrich my life and let more friendship appear."

"Ma, There's A Hobo At The Door"

By Tom Leech
©2015 Tom Leech

So there I was playing marbles in the yard,
With neighbor bud Joe (and I was winnin'),
And this guy wandered up the sidewalk,
Not to worry much 'cause he was grinnin'.

He had that look we kids knew well,
He was a hobo just strolling near,
Past our fence, and I gave a holler,
"Ma, there's a hobo headin' out here."

He never went onto our front porch,
If you went there you were sure to lose,
"Ma, he's headin' to the back door."
Hobos knew this was the door to choose.

Ma'd stop what she was doing in the kitchen,
And head to the back to greet the new one,
They'd trade hellos, then the hobo would ask
"Ma'am, you got any work you might want done?"

"Maybe weedin' the garden, mowin' the lawn?
Choppin' firewood, get the trailer unstuck?
I'd like to help out," the hobo would say,
(the idea was get hired and make a buck).

Or if Ma didn't need any help that day,
The hobo would easily understand,
And ask "Maybe got a goodie for me?"
Ma'd check the fridge and hold out her hand.

There'd be an apple or batch of grapes,
"Oh my, thanks very much," he'd often say –
They were always polite, cause that made sense,
And he'd munch a bit as he'd stroll away.

Sometimes when they rambled down the street,
We kids would tag along, over the lawn,
Curious and asking the usual questions,
"How'd you get here?" and "Where else you goin'?"

In our little town we knew each other,
Most likely he'd just hopped off the train.
(We had many freight cars runnin' slow,
So, hitting the ground took little pain.)

Then we'd head home to do more nothin',
Or have some fun tussling with our pup.
And just maybe see if Ma needed help,
Then goof off 'til the next hobo showed up.

Tackling Life's Early Dilemmas

by Tom Leech
Published in *2016 Oasis Journal*

How are you going to make it,
As a little kid growing up?
Life seems loaded with hazards,
And you're not much more'n a pup.

So where do you go for coaches,
Who'll head you down the right track?
Maybe if you had some gurus,
They'd fix where you lacked the knack.

The first thing you'll need is muscles,
Cause punks'l kick sand in your face,
And 97-pound weaklings,
The girls won't allow in the chase.

So cast your luck with Charles Atlas,
And you'll be making the right move,
Then you'll get muscles like Popeye,
That got him into Olive's groove.

Does that mean to eat more spinach,
Or chow down with cowboy Tom Mix?
And start your days with Hot Ralston?
Is that the way to get your kicks?

Where else can you get some good tips?
How about your pals at the pool?
They'll teach you Marco and Polo,
You won't learn that at grade school.

Radio might give you some key clues,
Do you go with sweet talk or force?
Because who knows what evil lurks?
Well, that Shadow guy knows, of course.

Then there's that really weird Whistler,
Who knows much as he walks by night.
Mainly beware those creaking doors,
Inner sanctums are a bad fright.

Heed Jack Armstrong, all American,
Do well and for sure, never cheat,
Just follow the Boy Scouts' motto,
And help those grandmas cross the street.

Look to the flicks to seek your coach,
Decide if it's giants or runts.
Would it be that Wile--E Coyote,
Or the Roadrunner's beep-beep stunts?

Do you go with Hoppy or Gene,
Or would Roy be a better course?
But when you're just a little guy
How the heck do you kiss your horse?

Kids Buying Bonds?

by Tom Leech
The Garrett Clipper, Garrett, IN 8/17/2015

"Buy War Bonds" were orders we all knew,
"Help us win this war," this WW2,
And most of us kids pitched in with real zest,
Helping our troops was our own special test.

So every week, whether rainy or sunny,
With paper boy or babysitting money,
We'd head to the Post Office on our journey,
Some of us so short we'd stand on the gurney.

The clerk greeted us with a friendly smile,
We'd plop down our coins in an eager style,
The stamps he gave us got our ardent look,
We'd paste them right into our War Bond book.

It was fun to see when those pages were filled,
The real Bonds we now got helped our passion build,
Our $18.75 aided our troops in their fight,
So let's keep buying stamps to add to their might.

Then one special day we heard big news arrive,
That was August 14, 1945,
The Japanese surrendered, the war is done,
After much struggle and strife, our troops have won.

Those "Buy War Bonds" posters had been the urge,
Yes, our dimes and quarters had helped the surge,
A decade later when the bonds would mature,
Those $25s back helped our next steps for sure.

Looking back at those efforts is worth a pause,
Investing our quarters helped that vital cause,
So maybe applying that process today,
Would help our kids see that investing does pay.

The Iceman,
The Milkman And The Mailman

by Tom Leech
©2010 Tom Leech

It was a special event when that truck rolled up
And we kids dashed over as if to attack.
We lined up with eager anticipation,
Waiting for the driver to walk to the back.

For this fellow was the iceman,
On his rounds to refill that special box,
Where Mom kept the ice cream and hot dogs,
Plus peanut butter, jelly, even ham hocks.

He'd chop away and break off a large cluster,
Then it went into that bag on his shoulder.
He'd stride out back and into the kitchen,
Then toss in the ice to keep the food colder.

The fun part for us kids, as we interrupted our play,
Was to catch the ice chunks as he'd chop away.
Wow, that was great fun during a hot day's romp
To grab hold of a sliver and slurp or chomp.

Another visitor was the early-bird milkman,
Who dropped off our bottles before we got up.
Then we could pour cold milk on our Wheaties
And maybe hand some on down to the pup.

On a hot summer day we'd better get 'em quick,
Or that milk would go sour in the heat.
When it got warm forget the Wheaties,
Though hot milk with cocoa was hard to beat.

In wintertime when we brought in the bottle,
That milk now had a different look.
Sitting there in the cold made the cream poke up,
So you could lift it right up with a hook.

Then there was that other handy fellow
With a different bag hanging off his shoulder.
He'd show up each day, come rain or shine,
Bringing postcards, letters, maybe a folder.

Our mailman was sure a lanky guy.
What else would he be as he trekked down the blocks?
He carried with him a sturdy stick,
To thump a mutt that might want to chew on some socks.

Now delivering the mail in Indiana
Was often not an easy task.
Fighting through that heat, rain, or ice,
Rarely gave time to relax or bask.

We often wondered just what he did,
When part way along he'd sure as heck have to go.
Maybe dropped that sack onto someone's porch,
And popped in to use the john and wave to the crow.

So this vital trio - iceman, milkman, mailman,
Helped us townfolk make our lives a whole lot better,
Bringing us fun and sometimes useful stuff,
Ice to chomp, milk that grows, maybe a love letter.

Slidin' down Milks Hill

(way back then and maybe still) by Tom Leech
From Garrett, IN Clipper 3/5/2009

The old hometown was low on hills,
So when that snow hit for more than a tad,
We kids would cheer and grab our sleds
And head over to the main one we had.

It was just a nothing much fancy hill
In summer or on into fall,
But come December to us grade schoolers,
Milks Hill gave a special call.

All of us kids knew Milks Hill well,
When snow hit we bunched up at the top
Staring at that slope heading down,
Ditching those warnings from Mom and Pop.

There we'd be with our sleds and sliders,
And a whole bunch of challenging jabber,
With terms like nuts, dare you and chicken,
Who was gutsy and who was just blabber?

The daring ones would push to the front,
With both hands tightly gripping that sled,
They didn't hardly have to trot at all
Flop runners on snow and down they'd head.

The rest of us would keep braggin' away,
Then Pete or Joe would get into place,
And off they'd go, followed by Red or Bill,
And soon it looked about like a race.

The aces would lie chest down on the sled
And steer smoothly to left or right.
Then when they hit bottom near Franklin Street,
They'd swerve, stop and hang on real tight.

Those not so skilled would sit on their sleds,
And a sidekick would shove them off.
Their mode of steering was with their feet,
Soon followed by crash, gasp and cough.

Say what you will 'bout those Garrett winters,
And there'd be lots of moaning against the chill,
But for my gang out there with coats and sleds,
It was hard to beat a day at old Milks Hill.

It's Scramble Time
When The Soot Hits The Sheets

by Tom Leech
From Garrett, IN Clipper 12/6/2010

Remember that rig we called the clothesline?
Where we'd hang those wet clothes out to dry,
After Mom had washed'm in the basement,
Wrung them out and in the basket they'd lie?

Then out back on the clothesline they'd go,
With white sheets spread out wide with their kin,
Towels, pants, socks and even some undies,
Hanging tight on the line with a pin.

And there they'd be spread out across the back yards,
Soaking in that sun on lines by the score,
Quite a sight if a breeze got the sheets waving,
Soon they'd be dry, fit for duty once more.

In winter those sheets wouldn't do much waving,
Tough to do when they're frozen stiff,
We'd haul them 'round like a flat piece of glass,
Once they'd thawed out, we'd fold 'em in a jiff.

But one event could transform this special scene,
One that'd link Mom and us kids like buds,
When we'd grab clothes baskets and unclip the pins,
Swiftly dragging down those wet sheets and duds.

You see, we lived in a railroad town,
Where locomotives would haul 'round the trains.
We'd hear whistles and see smoke rise above,
And even sing songs with jolly refrains.

The problem hit when one of those engines burped,
With not just smoke but a dark cloud of soot,
Which the breeze would carry all over the town,
Heading right where those clean sheets'd been put.

The word spread fast when that black cloud loomed nigh,
Neighbors'd be shouting "Big trouble's here!
Here comes the soot, get yourself afoot!
No, this is not the time to disappear!"

Mom would grab us kids and we'd dash out the door,
To haul down those sheets in one crazy scene.
If we didn't get 'em in there'd be a mess,
And back they'd go through the washing machine.

Going full bore, Mom would unclip those pins,
Swiftly tearing the clothes off the line.
We'd pitch them right down into the basket,
Not caring which duds were hers or mine.

It was really bad if Mom was at the store,
And about then a steam engine would blurt.
We kids would have to stop playing hide 'n seek,
Pulling clothes down's tough when you're just a squirt!

Finally came the day when new diesels arrived,
With steam engines retired among the treats.
We moaned a bit that those whistle tunes were gone,
But Moms rejoiced - no more soot on their sheets!

Shoes? Who Needs Shoes?

by Tom Leech
From Garrett, IN Clipper 9/15/2011

So there we were out on the streets,
Romping around with our chums.
It was summer in our small town,
Going barefoot wasn't just for bums.
(tho most of them did wear shoes)

We were just squirts, us girls and boys,
We'd ride bikes, play ball in the street.
Chase other kids down the alley,
Walk out to the pool, all with bare feet.
(who needed shoes there, anyway?)

Out on the farm, we dumped those shoes
As we slid around in the hay,
Brought in the eggs from those nasty hens,
Got scrubbed in the tub to end the day.
(and yes those feet needed a scrub)

We did have shoes, but those rarely showed,
For a wedding so we'd look real groovy,
When strolling over to Sunday school,
And walking uptown to the movie.
(Saturday afternoon specials)

Our feet were tough, that was for sure,
Just as tough as those real leather soles,
But wearing shoes gave us calluses,
Barefoot was good, lest you stepped on some coals.
(who'd figure that would become OK?)

Yesterday, a few decades later,
I tried again that fun barefoot style.
Off came the shoes and out for a stroll,
Cut short at five steps, not the hoped-for mile.
(call me a wimp, and you'd be right)

Saturday Night With The Monsters

by Tom Leech
From Garrett, IN Clipper, 3/29/2012

It was off to the Royal on Saturday,
In the afternoon or later at night,
Stroll uptown, grab your popcorn and settle in,
To see the latest flick, yes black & white.

Most times we'd cheer-on Roy or Gene,
Maybe even Hoppy on his winning streak,
Old Gabby made us laugh with that beard,
They'd leave us hanging to get us back next week.

But some nights it was a big change of scene,
From cowboys, ponies, guitars and songs,
To creeps and monsters, doing their nasty deeds,
We got caught up with aliens and Kongs.

There'd we'd be, urchins glued to the screen,
Watching mummies, wolfmen, zombies or their kind,
Dracula ready to suck out our blood,
Maybe even that newly-made Frankenstein.

Tightly, we sat, barely munching the corn,
Now with our fingers firmly gripping the seat,
Shrinking, flinching, gasping and gulping,
Even ready to flee to the outside street.

But mostly we managed to tough it out,
And as monster survivors, ready to roam,
We'd walk downstairs and out to Randolph Street,
Then over to Cowen for our stroll on home.

One night Pete and I were really spooked out,
And, as we walked, we kept checking with care,
In nearby bushes or behind a tree,
To make sure this night's monster wasn't there.

Was it lurking behind us or in front,
To the side, above, or behind that pup?
Would it sink its fangs right into our necks,
Take out our brains or just gobble us up?

So to spot them wherever they'd hide,
And make sure those evil villains we'd defeat,
Pete faced forward and I faced behind,
Walking back-to-back in the midst of the street.

We listened intently to hear those clues,
Breaking the stillness with "WHAT??? HUH??? SHHH!!! WHAZZAT???"
Those were our words we shrieked, whispered or gasped,
('til we saw the monster was only a rat).

But somehow we got home and darted inside,
Where – hallelejuh! – there were Mom and Dad,
Sitting on the couch, listening to the radio,
Maybe some hot chocolate soon could be had.

Except...now it was time to hit the old sack,
And if one of those creepies invades my dream,
I'll grow my own fangs and smack it with my pillow,
So I'll be here to see the next monster scheme.

I Never Peed In The Pool

By Tom Leech
©2009 Tom Leech

In my hometown summer meant hitting the pool.
For us kids it was many a splash and a flop.
Some could swim well, and others were dog paddlers,
A few swam underwater while most stayed on top.

One day the lifeguard pair, Buck and Rosie,
Rounded up our gang to give us some flack.
"Kids," said Buck, "We have a question to ask."
"Oh, what would that be?" we queried right back.

"We watch you all carouse out here for hours,
With summer nearly done and heading back to school,
We're baffled that you never hit the john,
Are you sure you're not going right here in the pool?"

Well, no one had ever asked us about that,
As I'm standing there soaked, trying not to drool,
"Well," I said, "I don't know about the others,
But I sure know I never peed in the pool."

"And so you'll know I wouldn't fib to you,
I'm showing how we Cub Scouts solemnly swear
That on my honor my answer is true,
With my fingers displayed and hand in the air."

Now lifeguard Rosie chose to get in on the act
And asked my chum Kat, sitting high up on a stool,
"How come we never see you going in for a break?"
"Well, same here," huffed Kat, "I never peed in the pool."

"OK," said Buck, giving chum Spike a dubious look,
"What's your line, kid? You gonna make like a dumb mule?"
"Geeze," sniffed Spike, giving him back an offended glare,
"I wouldn't kid you, I never peed in the pool."

Now Rosie switched over to her detective hat,
"That's so nice, Spike," then went on the attack.
"But when you're giving us such a heartfelt response,
Why are your fingers crossed behind your back?"

Spike, showing offense, defended his body style,
"You're just like our teacher, with her look aimed to fright,
And as I told her, it's just a medical state,
My fingers get swollen so I must squeeze them tight."

Rosie gave Kat another skeptical look
"Young lady, something was strange about your reply,
When your eyes peered away at something above."
Said Kat with a grin, "A bird up there caught my eye."

Buck turned to me and said he'd been a Cub Scout too,
Stating, with a glare suspicious to the core,
"Our pledges were done with the right hand, not the left,
And we proclaimed showing two fingers, not four."

"Well, there's a simple explanation," said I,
While giving him a sharp look of disdainful heft,
"When I swim, I hold my nose with my right hand,
So when you grilled me I forgot and raised the left."

So now you who are reading our tale of inquest,
Of lifeguards seeing if we'd broken some rule,
What's your story? Can you, as honestly as we,
Proclaim, "Heck no - I never peed in the pool!"?

HISTORICAL MOMENTS FROM MY EARLY YEARS

Saturday Bath On The Farm

by Tom Leech
From 2015 Oasis Journal

Out on the farm on a Saturday night,
We kids hauled water to the house from the well down the path.
With a bucketful balanced on each side,
This was the night we took the mandatory weekly bath.

No easy task, heisting those heavy pails
Up on the wood-burning stove and into a warming pot.
On the floor nearby, the round metal tub,
With a washrag, bar of soap, and stiff brush -- the whole darned lot.

Mom and grandma were the matrons-in charge,
Getting the next kid into the tub, filled with warm water.
Off went our duds and into the tub we went,
Made no difference whether uncle, cousin, son, or daughter.

There we sat in that old tub on the floor,
Mom soaping your ears and giving your back a scrub and scratch.
When Grandma dipped hot water from the pot,
That warmth on your skin was a feeling no shower can match.

Finally, scrubbed clean now, your turn was over.
Out you came, then grabbed a towel to use before you got cold.
Standing on the floor, naked as a bird,
Modesty's no big problem, not when you're just six years old.

But no hanging around, your turn was done.
On went your clothes, and then the next candidate drifted in.
And you headed out to the family room,
To the pot-bellied stove, where kinfolk played Old Maid or Gin.

Was there an order to the weekly bath?
Seemed no plan but there was wisdom in getting there early.
The first ones in got the freshest water,
And then -- yea -- you didn't have to follow Uncle Curly.

Ah, that felt so good to be freshly-scrubbed,
Wolfing down that popcorn, scratching the old Irish Setter.
Then singing some tunes round the piano.
What spa -- none that we knew -- could have done it any better?

When Peanuts Blair Was On the Mound

by Tom Leech
©2005 Tom Leech

He walked on out to the pitcher's mound
Though it was more of a slow stroll,
To try out a few warmup tosses,
getting ready to take his toll.

He was known to all as Peanuts Blair,
Advanced in years and large in size,
His pitches drifted rather than steamed,
So slow in pace they'd tantalize.

Peanuts was late coming on the scene,
The league had been around for years.
But he quickly showed them all his stuff,
Resulting in wild swings and tears.

The leadoff was a steady hitter
So astute he mostly got on base.
In came the first pitch; the bat whiffed air,
Look at that poor chap's baffled face.

For the ball had come in prime to hit,
So slow you watched it grow older.
Right at his waist when the bat came through,
It ended up by his shoulder.

The batter muttered and shook his head,
"How could I miss a pitch so slow?
I'll give this next one a healthy smack.
Now where the heck did that ball go?"

"Why can't I easily thump that ball,
Coming in at two miles an hour?"
Another arrived at that same speed,
Then one more swish and one more scour.

And now that ball was moving fast,
As the infielders tossed it 'round,
Hollering jeers toward the next guy up,
As he thumped his bat on the ground.

He glared out at Peanuts with a sneer,
"You lucked out on that last guy, Pop."
But his own luck soon deserted him,
As he chopped wildly at a drop.

The next pitch looked like an easy mark,
Yet his swing left nary a trace.
With a pitch so slow it barely moves,
How could he throw a change of pace?

The next one made the batter wobble,
And the crowd hooted with delight.
Why would he miss a pitch so tender?"
"It curved left and then it curved right."

So one more time the ball made the rounds,
As batter three stepped to the box.
This pitch ended up around his belt,
The swing way down near his socks.

The catcher strolled on out to the mound,
Was it for a strategy switch?
No, Peanuts had to take a breather,
After all, he'd tossed his sixth pitch.

Batter three exuded confidence,
He even waved his bat with verve.
Then his face showed he had been beguiled,
Was that a riser, drop or curve?

Just one more pitch could end this inning,
And one more batter seen to pout,
As he swung wildly in frustration,
"Stee-rike three!" was the ump's loud shout.

Now somewhere out there men are laughing,
But here it was a different sound.
Grown men were heard to mutter curses,
Cause Peanuts Blair was on the mound.

Baldy at the Bat

by Tom Leech
©2013 Tom Leech

It looked somewhat dismal for the Altona kids team that day,
The score stood 9 to 8 with but one inning yet to play.
The South Side gang was in the lead and displayed cocky heart,
Three more outs was all they would need for party time to start.

This was an empty lot 'til they made it a softball field,
Slicking it up with scythes they'd slung and mowers they had wheeled,
It soon fit the need, with bases firm and grass seeds they had sown,
And none were older than twelve in this new league of their own.

On the South Side mound was Tim, with maybe talent to flout,
He'd arrived in inning eight after starter Jeff wore out.
Infielders flipped the ball around, and hollered lots of chatter,
A style they spouted often, to hassle each Tony batter.

Tim's mode was underhand with a curve (tho more often not),
With only three more outs to get, he'd give it his best shot.
In this final inning, Flaky Flynn trotted to the plate,
Hits were not his style, but maybe one he could propagate.

The feverish crowd was jabbering as Tim slid forth the ball,
Flynn's bat came round, it nailed the pitch, and shot it toward the wall,
It climbed aloft and headed toward the clear blue sky above,
Then drooped on down to arrive in the shortstop's waiting glove.

Out One was made and now Bunty Blake headed to the front,
His name displayed his special skill, that was, of course, to bunt.
In came the pitch, Blake tapped it and scooted off with a burst,
Third baseman Juan scooped it up and his toss beat Blake to first.

The South Side kids whooped with glee as Out
Two had now been done.
Let's just get Spike the Sprite and it would be our time for fun. *
Spike's strikeout zone was small as he was only three feet tall,
And off he went to first when Tim's pitches all came in "Ball!"

The Clipper's scribe was recalling epic lines of verse,
About that Casey tale, where some Flynn had rounded first,
And then his teammate Blake had torn the cover off the ball;
Now hoping this Shrimp would get past first took a lot of gall.

OK, but no sweat, as next up was not even a boy,
Yes, a girl was striding to the plate, looking far from coy.
The South side blab was flowing strong with many spouting jeers,
Just one more out and they'd gobble up hot dogs and root beers.

Her name was Baldy, a nickname that didn't much relate,
She thumped the ground with her bat as she
stepped up to the plate;
There was ease in her manner and a tight grin curled her lips,
Though when you're only twelve, everybody's a bunch of pips.

Baldy was at the ready now to see what Tim would flip,
She eyed his pitch, smacked it hard and started it on its trip.
The fielders raced after it, that last Out to orchestrate,
But as it soared past them, Spike and Baldy both hit the plate.

Oh, somewhere in this favored land, the sun is shining bright,
And while no bands are playing, at least nine young hearts are light;
With a win of 10 to 9, those Tonys are prancing about,
But there's no joy on the South Side --
mighty Baldy "smacked it out."

Confession: there is some historic basis for this epic tale. Around 1948, when we were about ten to twelve years old, we Garrett kids put together our own softball teams (this was pre-Little League). We played on makeshift fields in different parts of the town - South, West, East, North, Altona, plus the Baptist Church. The author of this almost-true tale was the pitcher for the South Side team when Janet "Baldy" Zeider of the Altona team came to the plate and indeed did hit a home run. The pitcher has been reminded of that landmark event over the decades since. Baldy is well known for her many contributions to girls' softball teams over many years.

The Day Old Harry Came to Garrett

by Tom Leech
From the Garrett, IN Clipper 11/17/2008

"Well students," said Miss Dean to our class at the Will Franks school,
"We have a field trip for you, and this one's a real jewel.
A special visitor's coming, we're walking over to see.
The whole school's going, so let's all get in line and follow me."

So out we all went for a stroll toward the B&O station.
The fall leaves of '48 arousing our elation,
Others were heading there too, maybe a few from a bus,
And we waved at our Catholic chums, goofing off 'bout like us.

It was obvious where the train would be, so we didn't tarry,
The signs said, "Welcome to Garrett" and
"Railroaders welcome Harry!"
And there we were, lining the tracks when
that special train pulled in,
And we all started hollering, making one heck of a din.

A banner on the side proclaimed this the Whistle Stop Tour,
And the covered deck on back was all duded up for sure.
Some men in dark suits stepped out and gave us all
some serious looks;
Miss Gilbert said they were secret service, not some petty crooks.

We crowded 'round the back platform (a pretty fancy caboose),
And our mayor was there and said it was 'bout time to cut loose.
(We all knew Fritz and his words kids weren't supposed
to know or say
But we sure did, and we tried them out 'bout every other day.)

Fritz was a diehard Democrat as he was oft' proud to state,
Except the secret service someone forget to educate.
So they said, "To get up here, sir, you don't have a pray-er."
But some big shot said O.K. and on up went our mayor.

Fritz said our guest was known to some as "Give 'em hell, Harry!"
That fellow from the Show Me state, out there on the prairie,
(Though more recently the White House – that same place as many greats).
And out firmly strode the President of the United States.

Harry S Truman was his name though the S was only that.
He sure looked like a reg'lar guy, with his glasses and his hat,
(Dad had said he'd once sold them in a Kansas City store)
With a kerchief in his pocket, good-looking suit he wore.

With a big grin, he said he was thrilled to be in our great town,
And that having so many fine kids was a measure of renown.
For railroaders, this was certainly an essential resource,
With the longest mayor in history, a good Democrat of course.

I don't recall much else he said, but he said it good and loud –
Something about a do-nothing Congress seemed to stir the crowd –
And how vital it was to re-elect him and his VP,
A fine chap named Alben Barkley from down there in Kentuckee.

He didn't talk long but the cheers and shouts
were frequent and free.
Then he gave us one final grin and a hearty wave or three.
Then the train pulled swiftly away, headed off for several more
Of those same Whistle Stops on the way up to the Chicago shore.

The teachers gathered us up and marched us all back to the schools,
We were strutting, as the Pres had just said we were simply jewels.
Mr. Ober said we'd recall this when we were old and gray,
And Miss Cobler made it the class history lesson for the day.

Harry's opponent - Tom Dewey - in November failed to win,
Even though the Tribune headline said he'd won 'midst all the din.
But we kids knew why Dewey lost – he'd have to grin and bear it,
It didn't take much thinking; he just never came to Garrett.

(Note: historical accuracy not guaranteed; after all, I was only 12 years old. And if you're near Kansas City, MO, stop by the Truman Library, where the 1948 Whistle Stop Tour is a major topic.)

The Legend Of Emily Morgan:
The Real Yellow Rose?

by Tom Leech
©2014 Tom Leech

It was a day of glory for the General
As he rode slowly into the town,
Enjoying the rich accolades of victory,
Fitting for this man of high renown.

Santa Ana was relishing this day, as,
Those rebels had fought hard to defend.
The battles at the Alamo had been fierce,
But his troops had won out in the end.

Now another bunch of trouble was stirring,
At San Jacinto another fight.
A ragtag bunch claiming the name of Texans,
Going up against Mexican might.

Their leader was a fellow named Sam Houston.
With Jackson he'd fought battles way back,
Lately he'd seemed more an Indian than Texan.
Yet there he was now leading this pack.

But putting the crunch on that batch of Texans
Could easily hold off for awhile.
Santa Ana's troops might need some time to rest,
Relaxing to fit the General's style.

Now Santa Ana, though a good family man,
Was known to grab romance on the run.
So when most any day's battles were over
It was time for a good night of fun.

For the General it was often his habit
To choose a lovely maiden for play.
What better way to renovate his vigor
Than the joy of a roll in the hay.

And now with that Alamo mess concluded,
The General felt that urge for reward.
While eying maidens of various styles and hues,
A special one put spark in his sword.

Her look revealed she was likely a servant.
The General declared of no import.
"And what is your name," he asked this comely one.
"Emily" came her sparky retort.

She said Morgan was the name of her master.
Then, said the General with eye agleam,
"Emily Morgan, come sup with me tonight."
So this lady joined the General's team.

Now the General had put in some heavy days,
And Emily's style had tweaked his urge.
So he set his quarters on a nearby plain,
So eager was he ready to merge.

That night Emily shared well his bed and zest,
So well it stretched on to the next day,
With hardly either showing outside the tent,
They were wrapped up in intimate play.

Their passion extended to another night,
The tent shaking with each hearty ride.
His aides had not seen the General so taken,
And one more day of action inside.

But now the General's aides sounded an alert,
"Sir, a battle is looming ahead,
"And we're not well placed out on this open plain."
(Where our leader chose to make his bed.)

"We should move our tents and troops away from here,
So we're positioned to take up arms."
But the General replied, "I'm too busy now."
And headed back to Emily's charms.

Now Houston saw opportunity at hand,
And moved his troops to the better space.
Then he gave the word to charge that open line,
And the Texans roared out at full pace.

"Remember the Alamo!" was their loud shout,
As they attacked with rifle and lance.
Capturing Mexicans galore plus one tent
With one General in his underpants.

Was he a worn man as he stood defeated?
Was he chagrined as he passed his sword?
Did his dalliance with Emily prove unwise?
Did her efforts earn her a reward?

The San Jacinto win was the key event
That made Texas its own state that day.
And what of Emily who captured the General?
Rumors were heard that she'd moved away.

Now with her name on a San Antone hotel,
Was she a tart or woman of fame?
Who was the real Yellow Rose of Texas?
Say, was Emily Morgan the name?

Pair Up for Fame

By Tom Leech
©2014 Tom Leech

At the flicks we loved cartoons a lot,
Laughed at that coyote so cunning.
Wil-ee once more with a foolproof plot,
Roadrunner just beeped and kept running.

Many pairs made us laugh 'til we burst.
Laurel & Hardy trouble beckoned.
Costello wond'ring "Who was on first?"
While Abbott claimed "What was on second."

Some guys went alone for a shekel
Pairing up made more bucks with less pain.
Would Heckle have made it sans Jeckle?
And would Tarzan have swung without Jane?

The bad guys teamed for bucks and romance.
Jesse and Frank robbed just a few trains.
Many bankers met Butch & Sundance.
Bonnie & Clyde shot across the plains.

Bad guys watched out for a mounted pair –
Ranger with Tonto hot on their trail.
Cato sent Hornet off on a tear.
Batman & Robin would seldom fail.

From radio -- Atwater & Kent?
Lum & Abner jawed at the faucet.
Amos & Andy hustled the rent.
Moll groaned as McGee dumped the closet.

We learned about war in the trenches
From those scruffy pals Willie and Joe.
Giving laughter to lads and wenches
Bing & Bob on the road to and fro.

Fred solo might have made us aware,
But with Ginger he mastered the dance.
Bogie & Bacall made the screen flare.
Steve & Edie's songs made smooth romance.

TV's Sid & Coca gave us laughs.
Huntley & Brinkley brought us the news.
Desi & Lucy kept making gaffs,
Sanford & Son were always in stews.

Frankie & Johnny loved a way back.
Simon & Art bridged troubled waters.
Brooks & Dunn gave us the boot-scoot track.
Homer & Jethro were fun plotters.

Want coffee from just Sanborn, not Chase?
DNA took both Watson and Crick.
Max got Leo to Broadway embrace.
With Ben, Jerry makes ice cream that's slick.

Yes, Sony and Cher made a big split,
But who forgets Gleason & Carney?
So, try duos for sparkle and wit.
Lacking flotsam, jetsam's just blarney.

TALES ABOUT FRIENDS AND FAMILY

Strain Behind The Plate

**An epic poem, based on true historical record,
to mark the occasion of William Starner's 6th decade on this earth.
By T. F. Leech, who was there so it must be true.**

It looked extremely upbeat for the South side gang that year,
The team was stocked with talent that filled other teams with fear.
With Gris and Vanderbosch the right side was a snap,
LaRue at short and Potter third meant this team took no crap.

But the key to South Side's fortune, that made it percolate
Was that loudmouth, scrawny guy, Mighty Strain behind the plate.
All summer long the battles waged across the Garrett fields.
Those twelve year olds were fighting hard behind their various shields.

The West End showed a gamey bunch and East was seldom late,
But South Side held them both at bay, with Mighty Strain behind the plate.
The Baptist Church put forth a crew with guidance from above,
And from Altona came a horde that only mothers could love.

Yet as the season neared its close, South Side were almost champs,
The only challenge yet ahead was to thump Altona's tramps.
With South's enormous talent, seems a mild task to you,
But best not be too quick to cheer with Altonans three foot two.

The South Side team met at the mound, their minds to cogitate,
Then said "Why sweat it! We've Mighty Strain behind the plate."
The pitcher - Leech - and catcher - Strain - huddled in a rendezvous,
About the pitching smarts to use with batters three foot two.

The battle waged until the ninth, with South almost a cinch.
Their confidence was riding high with but three outs to clinch.
Leech asked his battery mate which pitch he next should hurl,
"Slider, fast ball, drop or spitter - which one's best to twirl?"

"Try #3." was Strain's reply, so Leech fired in one sweet,
Which Baldy, she of distaff make, popped onto Cowen Street.
"We're up by two, let's mop this up" came chatter from the field,
As Maggert One strode to the plate, clearly an easy yield.

"That strike zone's small," said Strain from behind the mask,
"Just put it there, into the mitt, it's just a simple task."
Eight pitches later, two Maggerts on, and neither needs a mentor,
To try for double steal, oops, catcher's throw went out to center.

"No fear," the infield chattered loud, "no reason to berate,
A momentary lapse, it's true, but Mighty Strain's behind the plate."
Another Maggert takes a cut and this one takes no sass,
His bat comes all around - hear Strain moan, "Oh my ass!"

Adding further insult, this tedious little runt,
Ends up on base while Strain danced round his tantalizing bunt.
Next one popped up - a very tricky curve,
"It's mine" said Strain, 'til he saw a redhead swerve.

Two Maggerts crossed the plate, and now the crowd did groan,
A Maggert hugging third could pull Altona home.
In steamed a pitch, a snappy drop, slipped by the catcher's scrote,
"Wild pitch!" whined Strain. "Passed ball." the scribes all wrote.

Oh somewhere hearts are happy, with kids a having fun,
But South hears muffled sobbing since Strain let in the winning run.
Now many years have dulled that scene, and Strain
may soon succumb,
But echoes still that clear refrain, "Replace that lousy bum!"

The end

P. S. Happy birthday Strain

Background. The time period is about 1948. Boys from various Garrett neighborhoods started their own kids' softball teams. Each team played on whatever local field they could use or develop, and soon, a league developed and games were played at Garrett's regular field by the pool. Baldy is Janet Baldy Zeider. In case you couldn't figure it out, this is a takeoff of "Casey at the Bat."

Tom Fleming Moves On

(memorial event 3/6/2005)
A few limericks
by his old pal, Tom Leech

Down on Tourmaline lived an old rogue,
Where a bachelor's life was in vogue.
To friends he'd often recite,
And his rhymes brought much delight,
Tho his limericks oft came with a brogue.

Tom was always precise in his speech,
With clear diction he really could preach.
Since he lived by the ocean
He'd lay more than just lotion,
So some called him a son of the beach.

For ladies our Tom was fanatic
With encounters often dramatic.
He romanced them round the globe
Even been known to disrobe
Females most prone to be Asiatic.

Now Tom headed above with the best
Where Gabriel said first pass this test.
"Tell us just one verse not 'X'
On something other than sex,"
Which is why Tom is now Satan's guest.

(Just kidding, folks)

Hot Curl – The Surfing Legend Of Windansea

by Tom Leech
From San Diego Magazine Outdoors Forum, February 2004
©2004, Tom Leech

It was 1963 and a character appeared on the rocks near the palapa at La Jolla's Windansea Beach, a surfer's haven. He would have a brief moment on that perch before the authorities challenged his right to be there, silent, looking toward the sea. Then away he went, except the local surfing and beach crowd, of which I was one, rose up and challenged city hall... and won. Back he came to a victory celebration on a day worthy of recognition and perhaps even a grand festival, July 14, 1963 (known to some as Bastille Day -- O.K. they can share it). His picture appeared in several publications, including San Diego Magazine. Some people talked of a run for mayor. He made a cameo appearance in one of those beach flicks with Frankie Avalon and Annette Funicello. Unfortunately some scoundrels did him in and that was his demise.

Except it wasn't. The legend lingers on. For years he's been seen hanging at a popular La Jolla restaurant. Grizzled beach vets bring him into conversations on occasion. Over at the former Hall of Champions Sports Museum in Balboa Park, he was a featured attraction for their surfing exhibition. And in March 2008 Curl took up residence at the California Surf Museum in Oceanside. So here is, five decades later....

The Legend of Hot Curl

At Windansea Beach around sunset time,
as the surfers start to wind down,
On the bluff will always be visitors, some locals,
some newcomers.
They know about Windansea and its delightful serenity.
They come for a special moment, when at dusk
the surf quiets a bit.

Old timers often speak of another who never missed a sunset.
He stood alone, a typical beach regular, peacefully gazing,
Bare-chested, toward the sea, absorbing the sounds,
the sights, the beach.
His name was Hot Curl, and those who knew him
would never forget him.

His hangout was next to the palapa, on the rocks just above
where the surf crashed at high tide.
He rarely said much; yet all knew who he was and
that this was his place.
Life was good for Hot Curl, just as for the others who
hung out at the beach in the early '60s.
Barefooted, floppy shorts, a mop of hair -- drooping --
maybe just out of the surf.

Where'd Hot Curl come from anyway? His background
always was vague.
Was he from the local high? Mission Bay? Wandered down
from Hoover or Helix?
Maybe even a transplant from some faraway place like
Indiana or Texas, not likely that one.
No problem. The locals were a tolerant crowd and
it took little to fit right in.

Curl sort of materialized, so to speak, from a favored
hangout a few blocks over.
There you'd see him with the gang at the Pour House,
on the boulevard.
An artist chap named Mike Dormer seemed to know him well,
There was even a sort of resemblance, a cool, casual, scruffy look.

Mike drew a bit even back then and he sketched old Curl
pretty true to life,
Not on the bar stool, but out on the bluff, at Windansea.
(That's the same Dormer who painted that wild crowd
at the Sip & Surf.
Which were real -- the ones in the mural or those reclining
by the boards?)

Another one of the bunch named Lee Teacher was a kind of
early image coach,
And he nurtured Hot Curl along and helped him develop that
laid-back style.
No one could ever say Curl wasn't a genuine product of the sand.
(No lack of role models hanging around there, or over at the ocean.)

Not exactly one of the super athlete crowd from the
not-so-slight paunch,
And with a half-empty can of cerveza, likely Dos Equis,
nestled in his left hand.
(Or was that his right and was it an Ole? No matter.) Doing what?
Being there, what else, what more? Always checking the surf,
the sea, the sky.

Catch those pelican skimming by, some frisky dolphins, the sport
fishers near the kelp beds.
The waves careen into the cracks in the rocks and slosh back out.
As sunset nears the colors richen and flare, then spread and
slowly fade.
Then it's dark and the moon gets its turn to make the place magical.

Hot Curl had his moment of fame, from his perch there
on the rocks.
When they sent out the call for some real beach guys and gals,
A bunch from right here – could you get more authentic? --
headed up to Hollywood,
And Hot Curl was there on the screen at that Muscle Beach
Party with Frankie and the chick.

Back at the beach, Curl, the regulars and the visitors watch the
hues blaze then ebb,
Some good rollers coming in -- oops, that board'll never be
the same.
No matter, life is good. You notice the chicks do sort of
gravitate here.
This is their place too. Takes a languid look to catch their eyes.
That's Curl, languid.
But one day Curl was not at his post. The palapa was missing
something,
The scene was not right. Hey, where's the man? Hot Curl?
Some said they'd seen him off Rosarito, even lounging on the
beach at San Felipe,
Surely he wouldn't have moved up to Manhattan Beach?
Not a chance.

No, Curl wasn't at any of these, at least it couldn't be proven.
Any chance some other legendary beach character got jealous
and turned evil?
A nasty rumor spread that he'd been evicted, that the fuzz gave
Curl the boot,
Off the rocks, no more hanging around at the palapa.

Well that didn't go over well with the regulars.
Tempers started to flare.
And all of a sudden a bunch of scruffy beach types and
even respectables

Were asking questions and squawking that somebody
overran their authority.
That if anybody belonged at Windansea, it certainly was Hot Curl!

Well the fuss hit the fan and the letters flew. And an army
marched on city hall.
Surfers, trim and grizzled, community leaders, art lovers -- yes
even they -- all converged
For the showdown; their impassioned oratory resonated through
the packed meeting hall.
And wisdom, or the oratory, prevailed. Curl got the O.K. to head
back to his perch by the palapa.

It was party time – it took little to get one going with this crew –
and the invites went out.
For the Sunday morning "Re-erection of Hot Curl."
(Were there hidden meanings there?)
Rejoice! Virtue has triumphed!" proclaimed the announcement.
It was an event not to be missed. Curl's photos, with surfers and
surfettes paying appropriate homage, made all the papers.

Well-done team. What not yet through? Hot Curl for Mayor?
Oh yes, the draft began.
And quickly died when the candidate did the same.
Serious wipeout. Done in.
By whom, you say? A fatal accident from an errant surfboard
and one of those giant waves?
A kamikaze pelican? Maybe even, dare I suggest it, homicide?
A mystery and sadness.

Now Curl was gone and he was sorely missed. Something was
lost at Windansea.
It never was the same. He wasn't exactly a model to emulate but
he personified the place.
It would gain some fame a few years later, when Tom Wolfe
wrote about the pump house,

A few rocks over from where Curl hung out.
Different gang, but not much.

Mike put Hot Curl to paint, did a right good job.
That's old Curl greeting you out there at that café on Prospect.
There's the palapa, the floppy shorts, the half-consumed
Dos Equis, or was that an Ole?
All you need to supply are the sunset, the pelicans,
the crashing surf.

Curl would be in his '60s now, the paunch a bit fuller
(those cervezas do add up),
Less of a mop to ruffle. Perhaps they'd call him Gramps.
He'd still show up at the palapa
Gazing serenely toward the sea, still that languid look,
still enjoying the good life.
And on the bluff, another one stands, looks at the lonely palapa,
and smiles.

There you have it – the true skinny on Hot Curl. Go check him out at the Oceanside California Surf Museum (www.surfmuseum.org) or the Spot on Prospect St. in La Jolla. Thanks to long time San Diego Magazine artist Mike Dormer, as you read an early close associate of Curl and illustrator of many of my articles, who helped refresh my memory. Mike passed away in late 2012.

Tom Leech is a long-time San Diegan, free-lance writer and author of several books. He was Editor of San Diego Magazine's Online Outdoors Forum, where this epic tale first appeared in February 2004.

Ah Those Memorable Beach Hangouts

By Tom Leech
**Appeared in the Guilded Pen, the 2013 Anthology
from San Diego Writers & Editors Guild**
©2005 Tom Leech

In those lively times called the Sixties,
For grub, friendships, music and fun,
Were the places where we'd often head
After a day of surf or sun.

On a Sunday from a day at the beach,
On the floor if you were able,
For a brew (or two) at the Sip & Surf,
Where a surfboard was your table.

Monday was a night to lay back
for some chat with a friendly guy or girl.
Just drift on into the Pour House,
With fellow beats, artists, maybe Hot Curl.

Don't miss Mantiki's on a Tuesday night,
Way over there on Midway Drive,
To hear rowdy folk songs going full bore,
With groups that were both loud and live.

Wednesday nights were fine at the pier
A dining bargain hard to resist,
Where a quarter got you dinner at Maynard's
And a beer with that since you insist.

La Jolla was fine on Thursday nights,
And gave your wallet only mild dents.
The Courtroom brought us special delights,
With spaghetti at just nineteen cents.

For a Latin guitar muy grande,
Along with some good Mexican food,
Off to El Sombrero on Thursdays,
Way before you'd be known as a "dude."

Friday night was happy hour time
Out on that Shelter Island deck,
The Voyager was the place to be,
To meet, carouse, or maybe neck.

Then later the must-stop-in locale,
Where some old and new friends you might see,
Yes, some called it a body shop,
Ah, those wild nights at MCRD.

On many a Saturday afternoon
The casual crowd in South Mission,
Just hanging around at the Beachcomber,
A scene like Lautrec, or yes, Titian.

Saturday night up at Bully's
With racy paintings on the wall,
For a juicy prime rib or steak
And intercourse not hard at all.

Sunday night and the week was closing
Last call before back out to work,
Perhaps one more drink at the Pennant
Whether pilot, techie or clerk.

Yes those were places of adventure
For a social whirl hard to beat.
For a few to forget Vietnam,
With memories vivid and sweet.

What's more awesome than a butterfly?

by Tom Leech
From the 2016 Guilded Pen anthology
of San Diego Writers & Editors Guild

When out strolling in the garden,
Or along a pathway in the park,
What will grab your attention
Is a butterfly with its instant spark.

How can it not capture your eye,
Transforming your stumbling and muttering,
With its colors that glow and glimmer,
And its flipping, flapping, and fluttering?

With those wings you can't help but watch
When they spread open wide as to soar,
Then flicker back next to the posy
For a touch, a quick sip, or maybe more.

Then darting with a move so quick,
Off to one more red or blue blossom,
While flipping, flapping, and fluttering,
Not much could be truly more awesome.

Well something brightens that image,
When you see a pack of eight or nine,
More flipping, flapping, and fluttering,
Brings joy for that flutterer that's mine.

Great Duos of History

By Tom Leech
©2003 Tom Leech

First came Adam & Eve, said the tale.
David gave Goliath a hard thump.
Where'd Jonah have been without that whale?
Delilah's trim made Samson a chump.

Romulus & Remus founded Rome.
Damon & Pythias liked to revel.
It's after you, Alphonse & Gaston.
Orpheous & Eury played the devil.

Romeo & Julie thrill girls and boys,
Though not Montagues & Capulets.
Later came the Hatfields & McCoys,
And on Broadway the Sharks & the Jets.

Would Don Q have won without Sancho?
Who was Ahab without Moby Dick?
Hyde had Jekyll for get out and go.
Dr. Watson helped Holmes look real slick.

Those tale spinners loved a good pairing.
The Bard gave Rose and Guildie bad luck.
The Grimms' Gretel kept Hansel staring.
Twain's Tom wove wild adventures with Huck.

Rob Peter to pay Paul for a thrill,
Is it Tweedledum or Tweedledee?
Head straight up the hill with Jack and Jill.
Join both Owl & Pussycat at sea.

Mapping the West were Lewis & Clark.
Vote Tippiecanoe & Tyler too?
Mason & Dixon's line set a spark.
Grant & Lee first made war and then woo.

Look at how artists matched up so well.
Like those great scenes from Currier & Ives.
Gilbert & Sully made music jell,
Rodgers & Hammerstein thrilled our lives.

So if fame and fortune is your call,
Find a good partner to help you share.
By going solo, you keep it all,
But "all" may be grander as a pair.

It's a Trio World

By Tom Leech
From the San Diego Writers & Editors Guild 2013 Anthology
©2013 Tom Leech

It makes me wonder as I contemplate life old and new,
When we arrive, it's solo; get hitched and we're up to two.
But the number that keeps appearing in tale, tube or game
Is so often a trio that's gathering the fame.

With Father, Son and Holy Ghost we reap what we shall sow.
In that fiery furnace? Shadrach, Meshach & Abednego.
How many wise men from the east were following that star?
Three atop those camels -- Melchior, Caspar, and Belthazar.

The threes were often there in the tales from writers and seers.
Who doesn't recall D'Artagnan and the three Musketeers.
Then 'ol Ulysses as he wandered 'cross environs
Was almost done in by that weird trio of sirens.

When Goldilocks dealt with a bear (or was it a llama?),
Not just one or two, it was Papa, Baby and Mama.
And sailing off in that wooden shoe (better'n a hot rod),
Heading out to see the world were Wynken, Blynken & Nod.

The Bard knew what it took to give us a case of twitches,
Brewing up toil and trouble were those spooky three witches.
The WW2 nasty 3 for grown up, kid or teenee,
We all knew them well: Hitler, Tojo and Mussolini.

In show biz, manic threesomes display their wacky cargo.
The ones who made us laugh were Groucho, Chico and Harpo.
And right there with them always cavorting and squirelly
Was that threesome of stooges. Yep, Larry, Moe and Curly.

In baseball Evers and Tinker don't even rate a glance.
But what a big cheer when it's Tinker to Evers to C⎯⎯⎯.
And golf fans know the trio that could always lure them back
For those epic battles between Arnie, Gary, and Jack.

You think of some as duos, say Bob and Bing on the road.
Yet when sarong-clad Dorothy arrived, that act really flowed
And right out there among 'em, cheering soldier and marine?
Who else? The Andrews Sisters -- Patty, LaVerne and Maxene.

Now why aren't there ever four tenors? Why's it always just three?
And who's that outlaw moaning about "Waylon and Willie and me"?
There are so many threesomes it's starting to get scary.
If not Crosby, Stills & Nash, it's Peter, Paul & Mary.

It seems whichever way you look, the threesomes do seduce.
<u>Look up</u> at Orion: Rigel, Bellatrix, Betelgeuse.
<u>Look down</u> when out hiking, ready from poison oak to flee,
You know the ones to look out for: avoid those leaves of three.

So you see we can get along without quartets or pairs,
Just as easy as having lunch or walking up the stairs.
But if it's not a threesome, it well should make you wary,
So come and join the team, like ev'ry Tom, Dick and Harry.

Quartets Abound

by Tom Leech
From The Guilded Pen, SDWEG 2016 Anthology

Back in school was this singer crew,
They warbled fun tunes when we kids met,
Harmony was their amazing style,
They called themselves the barbershop quartet.

It was fun listening to those singers,
We joined right in hearing those voices soar,
They made me think about other teams,
How many were around in groups of four?

On Sunday morning in Bible class,
As we learned life's lessons hither and yon,
We heard much from a heavenly four,
With stories from Mathew, Mark, Luke & John.

In history class, or was it in Lit?
We found enforcers who waved heavy whips,
They were Conquest, War, Famine & Death,
The Four Horsemen of the Apocalypse.

We'd tune up our radio volume,
Enjoying those groups with our Moms and Pops,
Quartets singing those current hot hits,
Four Aces, Four Freshmen, even Four Tops.

One time on that Ed Sullivan show,
He introduced a group called the Fab Four,
They also went by a different name,
The Beatles' success would soon really soar.

Another group of four were women,
They got many laughs on their TV show,
Known as Estelle, Betty, Bea, & Rue,
Those fun Golden Girls made the chuckles flow.

To see four of our famous leaders
And refresh your own historical lore,
Go see George, Tom, Abe and Teddy,
Carved up high on the rocks of Mt. Rushmore.

In life some go solo and that's okay,
And plenty of pairs are doing quite well,
Trios galore help us hum and pray,
And memorable foursomes ring the bell.

Nature the Rejuvenator

From the SDWEG 2017 Guild Anthology by Tom Leech

In this busy world in which we partake,
Often it's wise to take a long break,
Why not here in our San Diego world,
Where nature helps us to get unfurled?

To rejuvenate both bodies and minds,
Take in the super views in Torrey Pines,
For a place nature stirs surf, fun and reach,
Nothing's quite like a walk along Black's Beach.

Rather than flop down in a hot saloon,
Why not enjoy San Elijo Lagoon?
Or for a trek where water sometimes flows,
Pick a fun creek -- Tecolote or Rose.

Need some culture to add oomph to your spark?
Stroll through the beauty of Balboa Park.
When you want to put wind back in your sails,
Head for a hike in nearby Mission Trails.

Learn about history, advised your parson,
Explore Mule Hill with that dude Kit Carson,
And he'll be there again on workout hauls,
When you roam out to Penasquitos Falls.

When it's views and posies you're a scoutin'
Where's a better place than Iron Mountain?
And when your old bones are starting to creak,
That's your cue for a trek up Stonewall Peak.

With lakes, pines and peaks right off a byway,
Laguna's waiting off Sunrise Highway,
And for a ramble with many a tale,
Head way up north on Pacific Crest Trail.

Both coast and desert in San Diego?
Sure, head past peaks to Anza Borrego,
Split Mountain, Calcite Mine, gems to anoint,
And do you know what the heck is Font's Point?

Well those are some ways to enjoy pleasures,
Right near to home in our many treasures,
On foot, bike, mount, with pooch or Winnebago,
In our own special outdoors San Diego.

Presidio Park: How We Got A Fun Park For Free

by Tom Leech
From *The Guilded Pen*, SD Writers & Editors Guild 2019 Anthology

There was this hill, nothing fancy about it,
Though it was a good spot to view the near valley,
And over there was a wandering river
That made it a fun place to wander and dally.

Tribes of many names over the centuries
Had made this hill their village and gathering spot,
As history researchers in more current years,
Were able to learn from many a dug-up plot.

Here's where the Spaniards set up their mission,
With a padre named Serra the key to the ground,
Then they moved it east for an important cause,
That's where enough water could be much better found.

Others soon arrived here and left many marks,
Mormon brigades who marched over 2000 miles,
Sailors from American boats in the bay,
Plus a skipper named Stockton whose name marks the files.

The landscape was much like those nearby hillsides,
Until a businessman with a big store downtown,
A civic leader who'd run twice for mayor,
Saw it and said "Why's this not a park of renown?"

So George opened his wallet and bought the place,
Then found special nature designers to employ,
Creating meadows, orchards, foliage and such,
To make a real beauty for people to enjoy.

To tie in the hillside's historical links
He re-built that same mission from its past era,
And made a museum of major acclaim,
Named after that Padre Junipero Serra.

Then in 1929 the businessman
Gave this to us as a community landmark,
And made it a place the public could call theirs,
With the relevant name of Presidio Park.

Should you want to make a real-life connection
And receive a memorable and personal lift,
Go visit his home next to Balboa Park,
And say "Thank you, George Marston, for your special gift."

The Next Time Around – Transmigration

by Tom Leech
From *The Guilded Pen*, anthology of SDWEG, 2012

When your fade out time comes, is there a fade in?
When your ticker stops ticking, will there be more din?
Will you be off to hell or reincarnate?
Some say you'll see heaven, or perhaps transmigrate.

That one intrigues me-- your soul gets new flitter,
Check out as a human, check back as a critter.
But what would it be, if you could get to choose?
Would you crow loud at sunup or be one that moos?

What to be or not? Yes that is the question.
Is it "Go there" or can you make a suggestion?
A chum was reflecting one day on the seas
As he gazed at the creatures in a stiff breeze.

"Recall what I said, when we were out golfin'?
If I get a choice, mine sure would be a dolphin."
"Just look at that dandy. He's never in a rut.
What fun to soar upward and then flop on your gut!"

A shadow flashed by me, and caused me to gawk.
"See that chap circling, such pleasure to be a hawk!"
Friend Jack chimed in, chasing girls was his habit.
"My decision's easy, let me be a rabbit!"

For Lucy the lawyer, picking was no lark.
It's difficult to choose 'twixt snake, weasel or shark.
Given to reverie was our friend Myrtle.
"I like it quiet so return me a turtle."

With gossiping Cal, we all grin and bare it.
Said he, "My choice of course - come back as a parrot."
"This is my chance," said our cunning pal Jeeter,
To pay back some jerks, in my guise as a skeeter."

Chimed in our pal Shorty, "Then my turn to laugh,
To look down and sneer when I'm up there a giraffe."
Said artist Jose, museum insider,
"What a web I'd weave with the skills of a spider."

I'll take perverse pleasure and feel like King Tut,
Just poop and they scoop when I come back as a mutt.
Just soak in the mud, and light up your Zippo,
Birds pecking your itches, ah sweet as a hippo.

That got us thinking of the new lives we'd lead
If we could write our ticket to fill our new need.
Would you soar in the sky or slink through the mud?
Swim through the ocean or chomp away on your cud?

The decision's not quick, when choices abound,
Should you be a darned critter the next time around.
So what do y<u>ou</u> think, now Les or Hannibal,
When on your next shot <u>you're</u> back as an animal?

What's That Word Again?
How The Farm Boy Pursues The Chicks

By Tom Leech
©2017 Tom Leech

Perched up on his horse the farm lad reclines,
He cools down with the winds as his watch he re-winds,
From the pond a bass had given him a chase,
Now he's humming along with his deep vocal bass.

When across the pond he sees a slow goose,
It reminds him he's got to produce more produce,
Except for that hole he's got in his boot,
Fix it in a minute or is that too minute?

But look what he does when he sees those does,
He shuts down the sows and it's his wild oats he sows,
At the café he toys with his puny salad,
To call him an invalid would be in-valid.

When he pursues ladies, they often reject,
Could he be perfect if his manners he'd perfect?
One proven way to enhance his success,
Address her as madam. when seeking her address.

When a smack he got on his nose ballooned,
He first wound a bandage right over the wound,
Then to keep from making any more mess,
He'd compress the tissues to make a compress.

"Ouch," he moaned, "that sure enough makes me hurt,
Get me back to the desert, it's time to desert.
She may tear my skin but I'll not shed a tear,
For some quick pain relief I'll order me a beer.

"Out there I can wander just like a gazelle,
I sure am a rebel and it's time to rebel,
It's time to put an end to such abuse,
When she tosses me her refuse, I'll just refuse.

"Her next smack toward my nose I'll swiftly deflect,
For success on this project, I've got to project,
And seeing my charm she will surely relent,
With a lovely present I'll be there to present.

"Then again maybe I don't need a beau,
So to avoid a row, across the pond I'll row,
Getting back to work is a good opine,
I'll combine my gear and fire up the combine."

CELEBRATING OUR MODERN TIMES

The Seven Days Of San Diego Christmas

by Tom Leech
From Mission Valley News Dec. 12, 2014

On the 1st Day of Christmas
My True Love Gave to Me
A Sea Gull in a Palm Tree.

On the 2nd Day of Christmas
My True Love Gave to Me
Two Margaritas
And a Sea Gull in a Palm Tree.

On the 3rd Day of Christmas,
My True Love Gave to Me
Three Cold Cervezas
Two Margaritas
And a Sea Gull in a Palm Tree.

On the 4th Day of Christmas
My True Love Gave to Me
Four Quesadillas
Three Cold Cervesas
Two Margaritas
And a Sea Gull in a Palm Tree.

On the 5th Day of Christmas
My True Love Gave to Me
Five Beef Burritos
Four Quesadillas
Three Cold Cervesas
Two Margaritas
And a Sea Gull in a Palm Tree.

On the 6th Day of Christmas
My True Love Gave to Me
Six Enchiladas
Five Beef Burritos
Four Quesadillas
Three Cold Cervesas
Two Margaritas
And a Sea Gull in a Palm Tree.

On the 7th Day of Christmas,
My True Love Gave to Me
Seven Cheese-filled Nachos
Six Enchiladas
Five Beef Burritos
Four Quesadillas
Three Cold Cervesas
Two Margaritas
And a Sea Gull in a Palm Tree.
Adios and Feliz Navidad

The Night The Reindeer Stayed Home

By Tom Leech
©2010 Tom Leech

'Twas that night before Christmas, time for much prep,
But the reindeer sent Santa a legal rep,
Who came waving a contract and protest sign.
Now Santa was stuck, with that major deadline.

Santa had said, "It's almost the hour,
When we soar 'round the world on reindeer power,
Onward we go with my team and the sleigh,
Loaded with goodies for the kids' holiday."

But the rep said "Santa, it's this way, you see,
Better look at this contract, line E2Z –
Although it's time to hitch up the sleigh,
Your reindeer don't work on a holiday."

Santa was distraught on hearing this yarn,
That his reindeer would stay back in the barn.
"If the team I depend on won't come through.
Kids and their parents are likely to sue."

But when the rep stood firm and raised his arm,
Santa was nearing a state of alarm,
The message was clear "NOT WORKING TODAY!
When it's a holiday, reindeer just play."

The elves were worried about this game,
"Boss," said a wee one, Farley by name,
"We've huddled to see what else could be done.
We think we know how you can make your run."

"Well, what's that way?" Santa asked without joy,
Said Farley, "When we're not making a toy,
We ride motorcycles across the sky."
(He winked at the others with twinkling eye.)

"We ride on cycles that rarely stop,
And we've got some dandies here in the shop.
Let's hitch 'em to the sleigh and away we'll flee.
With Wanda, Little Rocky, Sy-Grumph and me."

"I'm game," said Santa, no longer dismayed,
As Farley and pals their choppers displayed.
"Let's show those slack reindeer what it's about."
Santa sprang to his sleigh and gave them a shout!

"HEAD 'EM OUT, FARLEY, ON THAT HARLEY!
GO LITTLE ROCKY ON KAWASAKI!
HIT IT, OLD SY-GRUMPH ON YOUR TRI-UMPH!
REV IT UP, WANDA, ON YOUR HONDA!"

So off they flew, like coursers they went,
With Farley's Hog, all hot on the scent,
They made all the rounds and dashed away all,
Those leather-bound elves were having a ball.

Their tasks now ended, 'twas a homeward race,
And there were the reindeer lined up in place.
"We've fired that rep," Dasher did sob,
"Next year we'll be your team for the job."

Said Santa, displaying a cheerful gleam,
"I've got too many kids for just one team,
So reindeer and cyclists, I'm glad you're both here,
Let's all celebrate with a holiday cheer."

"After such a long night, let's all hit the sack.
You cyclists did great and now we're all back,
So drive those choppers over to the dorm,
And take a snooze where it's cozy and warm."

"But before we wrap it up for the night,
Let's try it again so it goes just right.
I've had such a ball, belting out that fun rhyme,"
And he shouted with glee, one more jolly time...

**"HEAD 'EM OUT, FARLEY, ON THAT HARLEY!
GO LITTLE ROCKY ON KAWASAKI!
HIT IT, OLD SY-GRUMPH ON YOUR TRI-UMPH!
REV IT UP, WANDA, ON YOUR HONDA!"**

Deck the Halls – the Kitchen Calls

A little nudge about our Christmas dinners,
and you can sing along too.
by Tom Leech
©2013 Tom Leech

'Tis the season for the belly,
Fa la la la la, la la la, la.
Eat more buns with lots of jelly,
Fa la la la la, la la la, la.

Don ye now your tight apparel,
Fa la la la la la la la, la.
Feel your tum, now big as a barrel,
Fa la la la la, la la la, la.

See the growing blob before us,
Fa la la la la, la la la la.
Eat more cake, apples just bore us.
Fa la la la la, la la la la.

Stretch your tape in sorry measure,
Fa la la la la, la la la la.
While I seek out more pie pleasure,
Fa la la la la, la la la la.

Don't fast as the old year passes,
Fa la la la la, la la la la.
Hail your new grown chins and asses,
Fa la la la la, la la la la.

Munch we joyous, all together,
Fa la la la la, la la la la.
Bellies stretch, they're just like leather,
Fa la la la la, la la la urrgghh.

The Ode to Murphy

by Tom Leech
©1982 Tom Leech

A compendium of mostly true snafus that
have occurred to many colleagues.
They laugh about them now. They didn't at the time.

It's away to Washington for a major pitch,
A Winning Presentation and they'll all be rich.
They've busted their fannies to lay out their story,
They're loaded for bear, Brand X better worry.

The team of four aces, came together at two,
Was sabotaged early by the Asiatic flu.
Joe arrived looking green and lurched back on the plane,
Anne's charts came up missing, with the luggage again.

But the show must go on, the general won't wait.
So the rest of the team ran for the interstate.
But Avis said "What car?" and Hertz said the same.
"Hey taxi, over here, get us out of this rain."

Finally at the Pentagon, half an hour late,
Mac's clearance has lapsed, he's stuck at the gate.
The team's last two members, polishing their boots
Dashed to Conference Room A, in their power suits.

"Oh no, no one's there! How can that be?"
Simple, they're all waiting in Conference Room C.
To C they then headed, by now a bit whiffy,
"Turn on the projector, we're on in a jiffy."

What projector? There's none to be seen!
"Didn't you?" whispered Anne. "I thought you . . .," said Dean.
A projector arrived. "Let's go!" came a shout.
But 'twas not yet to be, the bulb was burned out.

Patience was fading as a new bulb was found.
Now the show did commence—oops, chart upside down.
Dean moved through the data, waving pointer with zest,
One swoop pitched hot coffee on the general's vest.

Anne then took the floor for the final appeal,
One nifty demo the proposal would seal.
First sparks, then much smoke—yep, incorrect power.
The general was drenched by the sprinkler's shower.

Later Anne and Dean, joined once more by Mac,
Cried in their beer, "We'll all get the sack!"
The moral is clear, as in that old saw:
Remember the power of old Murphy's Law.

From *How to Prepare, Stage & Deliver Winning Presentations*, **2nd Edition** (AMACOM) by Tom Leech.

Getting The Straight Poop For Those Special Reserved Seats

Press item: "U.S. MILITARY PAYS $6000 PER TOILET SEAT"
by Tom Leech
©2009, Tom Leech

The Senator was outraged when his aide showed him the costs.
"Surely that can't be true! You must be a decimal point off."
"No sir, $6000 per seat was in the contractor's bill."
"Well, that much for one toilet seat is enough to make one scoff."

"And now it's made the headlines and my constituents are irate,
How could our Air Force spend six thou for one crummy seat?
So clarify to me how that outrageous cost was achieved,
To make each seat that expensive had to be some mean feat."

"Is that throne made from rare marble or perhaps even of gold,
Or was the design tailored specially fit for use by a duke?
What the heck was in that contract that drove those charges so high?
Now the taxpayers are spouting that's enough to make them puke."

"Or is it trimmed in muskrat fur or warmed with solar power?
Then maybe each seat was specifically carved from precious teak,
Or are they bullet-proof to protect buns from sniper's attacks?
Or radar-protected so no enemy could sneak a peak?"

"And I'll bet they didn't hire from the regular labor force,
But artisans from the old school, so each is a work of art,
Wait, I'll bet it's in the Environmental Protection Act,
With output to be recycled plus a filter for each fart."

"Did they include hi-fi to help fighters enhance their relief,
Or with spigots to give each producer their own slug of rum?
Or perhaps -- I'm reaching now -- do these adjust to the sitter,
To add comfort by shaping the top to fit each person's bum?"

"Well," said the inquisitor, "Now I'm definitely pooped,
This search is exhausting and my energy is nearly drained,
Go off and bring me numbers to get the press off my back,
And I'll have answers so my voters might be a bit restrained."

A day later the numbers expert came back with the story.
"Sir," he said, "We've found what added to the liability.
It's a line buried in contract section 24 C9,
To place deluxe toilet seats in each Senator's facility."

The Senator was outraged when his aide showed him the costs.
"Surely that can't be true! You must be a decimal point off."
"No sir, $6000 per seat was in the contractor's bill."
"Well, that much for one toilet seat is enough to make one scoff."

"And now it's made the headlines and my constituents are irate,
How could our Air Force spend six thou for one crummy seat?
So clarify to me how that outrageous cost was achieved,
To make each seat that expensive had to be some mean feat."

"Is that throne made from rare marble or perhaps even of gold,
Or was the design tailored specially fit for use by a duke?
What the heck was in that contract that drove those charges so high?
Now the taxpayers are spouting that's enough to make them puke."

"Or is it trimmed in muskrat fur or warmed with solar power?
Then maybe each seat was specifically carved from precious teak,
Or are they bullet-proof to protect buns from sniper's attacks?
Or radar-protected so no enemy could sneak a peek?"

"And I'll bet they didn't hire from the regular labor force,
But artisans from the old school, so each is a work of art,
Wait, I'll bet it's in the Environmental Protection Act,
With output to be recycled plus a filter for each fart."

"Did they include hi-fi to help fighters enhance their relief,
Or with spigots to give each producer their own slug of rum?
Or perhaps -- I'm reaching now -- do these adjust to the sitter,
To add comfort by shaping the top to fit each person's bum?"

"Well," said the inquisitor, "Now I'm definitely pooped,
This search is exhausting and my energy is nearly drained,
Go off and bring me numbers to get the press off my back,
And I'll have answers so my voters might be a bit restrained."

A day later the numbers expert came back with the story.
"Sir," he said, "We've found what added to the liability.
It's a line buried in contract section 24 C9,
To place deluxe toilet seats in each Senator's facility."

Where Does Santa Go?

By
Tom Leech
From *Titillating Tales from the Outhouse*

So, tell me again, Grampa, about that Santa guy.
You say he flies all the night long, all over the place,
And then he pops down chimneys, I don't know how nor why,
Leaves toys, grabs milk and cookies, then he's off like a race.

Well, Grampa, one thing puzzles me, it's just got me miffed,
When he's out there all that time, something I'd like to know,
Is hour after hour, unless he's smart or swift,
Just tell me please, how, when and where does old Santa go?

I know what happens to me, and all the pals I know,
After slurping lots of milk 'n munching more'n one snack,
Is somewhere along the way we've just all got to go,
At school, in our john at home, or behind a bush out back.

I know I shouldn't let that stuff trouble me or you,
But I picture him with his fanny perched off the sleigh
And going number one or, my gosh, old number two,
As he flies over some poor little kid's dinner tray.

Whether it's us little kids or that old Kris Kringle
The teachers said not to leave a mess or pollute.
So, I'd hate to think he's peeing right on our shingle,
Or out over the rail doing a flying salute.

And what about the TP? Or corncobs in the woods?
You taught us to flush or bury the residue.
We've all learned just how and where to get rid of the goods,
But it still baffles me, just what does Santa do?

Grampa put on his thinking look, so he wouldn't flub,
"Well Joey, young laddie, since you put me on the spot,"
Tilting his head a bit and giving his chin a rub,
"I can tell you about how Santa uses a pot."

"When he's laid out those gifts, there's no time to say hooray,
He just tweaks his nose and poof, he's back up with his bag.
And when that urge hits Santa, he just can't stop that sleigh,
No time to dawdle, nor read the North Pole Daily Rag.

"You see, what they show of that jolly chap and his team,
Is the front part of the sleigh, with lots of toys in back,
All colorful and neat or at least so it would seem.
But what you don't see is the sleigh towing a small shack.

"The door has a slot, and there's a vent out from the top.
And inside is a one-hole spot on which he can perch,
So he won't need some person's house for that crucial stop,
(Even with warm seats, smooth paper and late news to search).

"That outhouse in the rear is Santa's private potty,
A very important part of the whole entourage.
A tweak of nose, a quick sit, and a refreshed body,
While the reindeer go off toward the next roof or garage.

"So, Grandson, now you know how Santa has worked it out."
Perched on his dear grandpa's lap, Joey nodded just so,
"Now I see that he uses that shack he hauls about.
But Grampa, wait a minute, then where does *Rudolf* go?"

end

THE WORLD
WE LIVE IN,
PLUS OR MINUS

Adding To Your Communication Success: Per The Bard's Tips

Created by Tom Leech

If shyness is part of your nature,
Seldom saying why *you're* the best to choose,
Now's the time to tout your *own* talents,
And ***"Be trumpet of (your) own virtues."***
Much Ado About Nothing

When engaged in a conversation,
And to blabber or listen is your choice,
A useful motto to adhere to?
"Give every man thy ear but few thy voice."
Hamlet

When your words seem to make little sense,
And your listeners wonder if you're not on meth,
Put your brain in gear before thy mouth:
"Weight thy words before thou givest them breath."
Othello

When someone has treated you nicely,
And they're not so high in your ranks,
How 'bout that oft-neglected statement?
"I can no answer make but thanks."
Twelth Night

When you're dining at a peaceful café,
And you feel inclined to blab on your cell,
Revisit, or you'll stir fellow diners
To shout **"Silence that dreadful bell!"**
Othello

When you're faced with a tough situation,
And deciding has got you in a stew,
Remember a valuable pathway,
Above all, **"To thine own self be true."**
Hamlet

And if your belly's got butterflies
And your words don't seem ready to flow,
Focus your thoughts toward the positive,
"All things are ready if our minds be so." *Henry V*

Now your team's worked hard to win one,
And your players are feeling their oats,
It's great when the boss sings high praise:
Yes -- **"Thou are the best o' th cut-throats."**
Macbeth

Hawaii Workout: (Oral Exercise)

By Tom Leech
©2002 Tom Leech

Head out from Honolulu, along Likelike Circle.
Look up to Puu Kanehoalani, around on Kamehameha.

Look for menehunes at Puuomahuka, and big Kahunas
gazing toward Healeakala and Kialakahua.

Pass the famous beaches of Kahanamaku, Makapu'u
and Nahonani. Come back onto Liliuahulani.

Shop at Ala Moana, pay homage to Duke Kamahameha.
Relax at Kahaloa and you're back in Waikiki.

Golf And English Are Tricky Games

by Tom Leech
From *The Guilded Pen* 2018 SDWEG Anthology

At our lodge over by the gulf,
We love to play that fun game of golf,
The course is right there by the beach,
Past that tall tree we know as a beech.

Before our game we sip some tea,
It helps us focus at that first tee.
Tactic one is to stop and pray --
Dear Lord help us whip that other prey.

Golf often comes with a "whether,"
It's hard to tell with nature's weather,
One thing for sure we're never bored,
Can't say that when we meet with the Board.

On the course the question is "would,"
Hit with an iron or better with wood?
Smack it wrong and you've bought your bier,
Sink it just right and slurp up their beer.

Lunch is when -we gather to meet,
And gobble down fish & chips or meat,
A treat is when our chums we bruise –
They have to pay for mugs of fresh brews.

Now pay the bill, a standard rite,
First make sure the numbers add up right,
Same guy always gives us our check,
His name is Jose, he's not a Czech.

Next round up as a go-cart passed,
Ready to play with some lessons past,
With golf some are against or for,
But all love to shout that neat word "Fore!"

Ode To A Titian Urn
(Or Let's Hear It For The Chamberpot)

By Tom Leech
From Oasis Journal 2017

At Grandma's, as the day moved to a close,
The kids of the clan headed up to bed.
The females took the bedroom to the right,
The left for Jake and me and cousin Fred.

Grandma and Grandpa had their room downstairs,
And Uncle Ralph got the room by the back.
We'd had supper, played Hearts, War, or Euchre,
Now we all were ready to hit the sack.

You could hear the wind whistlin' outside.
Brrr, it was winter in Indiany.
Thank goodness we had these warm covers,
Without them for sure you'd freeze your fanny.

For a while we told jokes and scary stories
And listened to giggling from across the hall.
But it wasn't long before our eyelids drooped,
Then it was just snoozing by one and all.

But then a bit later one of us'd stir–
It was nature's call – now who had to go?
You'd mull it over and think maybe not you,
But soon the need really would let you know.

Now Grandma's farmhouse had no plumbing inside.
We knew where the path to the throne room led,
To that little old shack out the kitchen door,
A short walk over by the chicken shed.

Brrr, it's freezing here, is that my only choice?
To leave that warm bed, head out into the sleet,
With an old overcoat and pair of galoshes,
Then dash, not walk, out to that ice cold seat?

No – 'cause each room had a chamberpot,
Kept under the bed and always ready.
When the need hit, there was the answer,
Slide it out, then make sure you were steady.

Our pot had a neat painting on the side,
From an artist whose name we'd come to learn;
Mom said he was a famous Italian
So of course we called it our Titian urn.

Nothing was better than that Titian urn.
You did your duty, shoved it 'neath the bed,
And crawled once more under those warm covers,
Then back to dreamsville was where your mind led.

Almost asleep, then comes that sound we know,
From next door a cousin slips from her sack,
Responding to that same essential call,
Then creaking bedsprings as she heads on back.

Come next morning and good old Uncle Ralph
Got the pot-bellied stove fired up.
We'd jump out of bed and into some duds,
Slurp some hot chocolate from a cup.

Then one of our chores was to carry our pot
Over to that little shack by the shed.
And we'd empty the collection from the night,
Scrub it and slide it back under the bed.

Then all day we ignored the chamberpot,
But we knew it surely would get its turn,
When once again as we all hit the sack,
And proclaimed "Hooray for our Titian urn."

They're Better Than Us – Hah!

By Tom Leech
©2010 Tom Leech

'We're totally superior to you!"
Proclaimed that bunch of wall-posted banners,
Spouting that those with purple skins,
Are way better than all other manners.

There's that bragging gang who often honk,
That there'll be no one else around but them,
Who'll have more lives once others conk,
'Cause only *their* religion's the true gem.

Well, I'm now here to plant the seed,
Who are the obvious superior ones?
And that's *my own* tribe, gang, and breed,
'Cause we have the better daughters and sons.

Some claim their skin color is dearer,
Wrong – ours is the only one not obscene,
Tops is what we see in *our* mirror,
That of course being our best-of-all GREEN.

Those people from those other nations,
With their ways so blatantly obnoxeesh,
They stretch our American patience,
And most of them don't even speak English.

Then there are those bums that speak with a drawl,
From Virginny, Texas or Alabamy,
And those snoots from Bahston or Idahawl,
I speak clearer than them wearin' my jammy.

It's so obvious my sex is best,
We're way superior to that other breed,
So we're freely the much better dressed,
Covering up is what those others need.

We've been told by God much more than thrice,
Only our religious types, per his dictate,
Will get to enter God's paradise,
All the others will meet a terrible fate.

Well, could there be a better sequel?
Would it be wiser to heed some truer voice?
Who said "We're all created equal"?
Maybe quit spouting that "I'm the superb choice." ?

Wait, before I get too carried away,
Recall those early dudes did not write down "WE,"
But "ALL MEN" was what they really did say,
So maybe I'm right to tout HE over SHE!

That's all, folks

www.ingramcontent.com/pod-product-compliance
Lightning Source LLC
LaVergne TN
LVHW091531070526
838199LV00001B/12